Geologic Ages and Events

Time BP	ERA/Epoch		Life Forms	Geologic Developments
5000	ATONAL		Rocks	Mountain ranges upthrust; continents form
3000	CATATONIC PROPHYLACTIC	} PRECOCIOUS	Ugly green slime Ugly green slime with orange spots	Earthquakes and volcanoes Volcanoes and earthquakes
	ORTHOPEDIC			
505	Accordion		Seashells	Torrential rains
425	Pedestrian		More seashells	Thunder and lightning
360	Freudian		Slimy things	More rain
325	Artesian		Slimy things with tentacles	More thunder and lightning
280	Pestiferous		Nasty crawly things	Rain, 40 days and 40 nights; oceans form
230	Obstreperous		Lots of nasty crawly things	Rain, with intermittent volcanoes
	METATARSAL			
205	Cryptic		Big warty things	Swamps form
165	Styptic		Really big warty things	Hot, with frequent rains; drifting continents
135	Creosote		Warty things too big; start over	Even hotter, with lots of mosquitoes
	CRETINOUS			
75	Obscene Uglyscene		Little hairy animals Big hairy animals	Cooler, with a 20% chance of comets Windy; small continent warning
39	Vaseline		Animals with silly-looking horns, ridiculous teeth	Cold, with night and morning glaciers
28	Listerine		Animals who don't understand about tar pits	Fair inland, patchy fog near the coast
12	Ovaltine		~~Shree trews~~ ~~true shees~~ ~~shoe trees~~ tree shrews	Warm and sunny; great weekend for a barbecue
1	Plasticine		First homonyms	Smog alert
25000 y	Recent		Modern person; first Republicans	Freeways upthrust; suburbs form
15 min	Very recent		First computer nerds	Fast-food chains form

millions of years

Science Made Stupid

Written and Illustrated by Tom Weller

Houghton Mifflin Company • Boston •

Library of Congress Cataloging in Publication Data

Weller, Tom.
Science made stupid.

1. Science—Popular works. I. Title.
Q162.W45   1984   500   84-12938
ISBN 0-395-36646-1 (pbk.)

Printed in the United States of America

M 10 9 8 7 6 5 4 3 2

Contents

Introduction

SINCE THE DAWN OF TIME, MAN HAS looked to the heavens and wondered: where did the stars come from? He has looked at the great diversity of plants and animals around him and wondered: where did life come from? He has looked at himself and wondered: where did I come from?

Later, he began to ask more complicated questions. He looked in his wallet and asked: where did my paycheck go? Am I on the right bus? Who do you like in the Series?

To the former questions, at least, science has provided answers.

What Is Science?

Put most simply, science is a way of dealing with the world around us. It is a way of baffling the uninitiated with incomprehensible jargon. It is a way of obtaining fat government grants. It is a way of achieving mastery over the physical world by threatening it with chaos and destruction.

Science represents mankind's deepest aspirations—aspirations to power, to wealth, to the satisfaction of sheer animal lust.

The cornerstone of modern science is the **scientific method.** Scientists first formulate **hypotheses,** or predictions, about nature. Then they perform **experiments** to test their hypotheses.

There are two forms of scientific method, the **inductive** method and the **deductive** method.

INDUCTIVE	DEDUCTIVE
formulate hypothesis	**formulate hypothesis**
⬇	⬇
apply for grant	**apply for grant**
⬇	⬇
perform experiments or gather data to test hypothesis	**perform experiments or gather data to test hypothesis**
⬇	⬇
alter data to fit hypothesis	**revise hypothesis to fit data**
⬇	⬇
publish	**backdate revised hypothesis**
	⬇
	publish

**Roger Bacon
(or Francis Bacon)**

Science as we know it today owes a great debt to a man named Francis Bacon, or perhaps Roger Bacon, or both. It is a debt seldom acknowledged, as few scholars wish to risk public embarrassment by confusing the two. Such concern is unnecessary, since the important facts are nearly identical.

Francis (or Roger) Bacon was born sometime between 1212 and 1561. Of both humble and noble birth, he rose quickly but slowly through the ranks of the Franciscan order, becoming Lord Chancellor under James I.

Bacon's contribution lay in his criticism of the Scholastic philosophy, which held sway in the Middle Ages (and Renaissance). In its place he advocated the direct observation of nature, or "inductive method." This radical departure was to bear fruit with the triumph of modern experimental science one through five hundred years later.

**Francis Bacon
(or Roger Bacon)**

Roger (or Francis) Bacon wrote a large body of works with indistinguishable Latin titles, which for that reason are no longer read. He died circa 1292–1626 while attempting to invent frozen food, gunpowder, or the submarine.

Many believe Bacon to be the true author of the works of William Shakespeare, or perhaps Bob Shakespeare.

Science for Everyone

Sound simple? It is.

Once, when the secrets of science were the jealously guarded property of a small priesthood, the common man had no hope of mastering their arcane complexities. Years of study in musty classrooms were prerequisite to obtaining even a dim, incoherent knowledge of science.

Today all that has changed: a dim, incoherent knowledge of science is available to anyone. Popular science books—with their simple, fatuous, and misleading prose, their garish four-color illustrations, their flimsy modern binding—have brought science within the reach of anyone who can afford their inflated prices, or wait a couple of weeks for the remainders.

Indeed, today a myriad of books is available that can explain scientific facts that *science itself has never dreamed of.*

This is one of those books.

1. The Universe

Pictures in the Sky

The ancients looked at the heavens and saw the shapes of gods and animals in the stars. This was probably due to widespread drug abuse in ancient times. Nevertheless, we still use the names they gave the constellations.

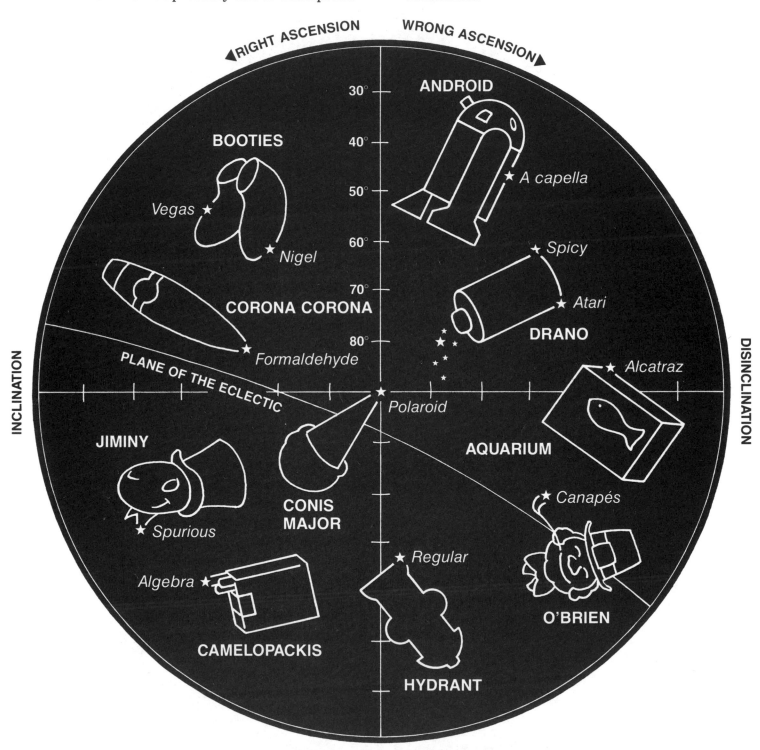

Constellations Visible from the Northern Hemisphere

The Origin of the Universe

The universe began five million years ago with the **big bang.** All the matter in existence, which had been compacted in a tiny ball, explosively flew apart. No one knows what caused it, but kids playing with matches is suspected.

As the primordial matter spread out, it began to coalesce into the celestial objects we know today—galaxies, stars, planets, and dust bunnies.

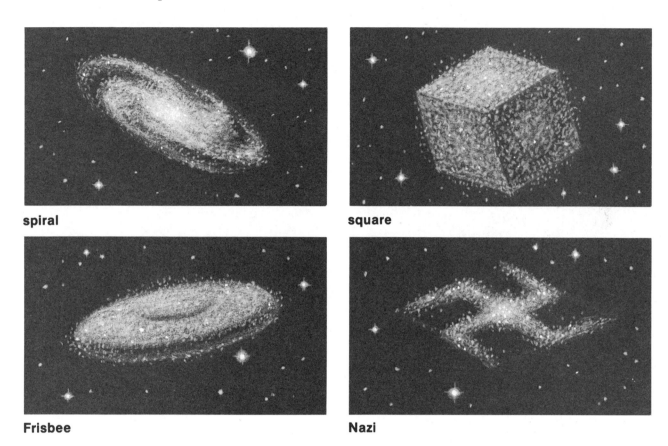

spiral

square

Frisbee

Nazi

Types of galaxies

Even today, the stars and galaxies continue to fly apart. This produces a phenomenon called the **red shift.** The further away a celestial object is, the more it appears to astronomers on earth to be shifted toward the red end of the spectrum.

"Red shift" shows increasing totalitarian domination of the outer reaches of the universe. Write your congressman! ▶

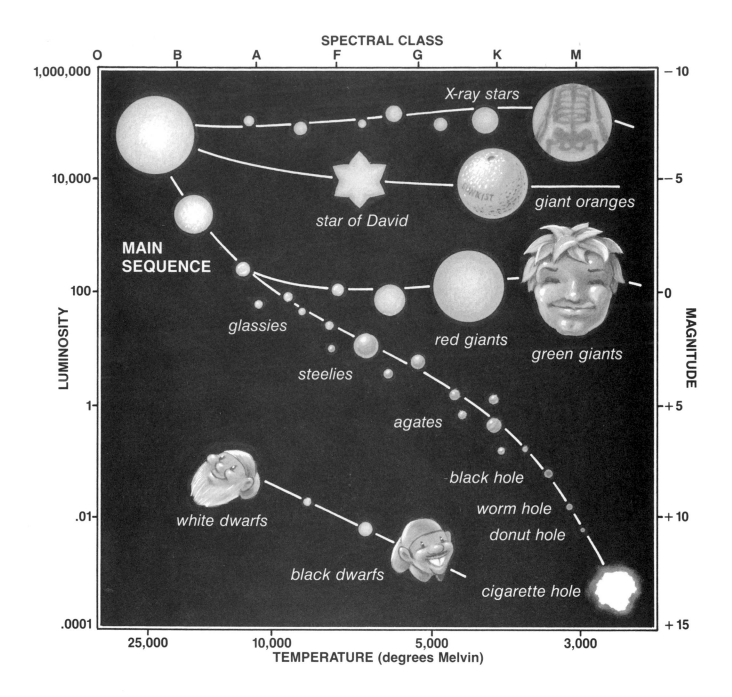

Stars

Stars are of different sizes and classes. They have a life cycle, just like living things. Young stars are called **starlets.** A star that has become very large is a **superstar.**

Stars are actually giant nuclear power plants. That's why they sometimes blow up—or go **nova**—just like the nuclear power plant in your neighborhood.

The **Rumpsprung-Hustle diagram** shows the various classes of stars.

Black Holes

When the interior of a star reaches a density a thousand times greater than the densest material known on earth—bagels—gravity causes it to collapse to an infinitesimal point. This singularity in space is called a **black hole**.

EVENT HORIZON

LIMBO

ESCROW

FRESNO

HAND WASH
·DRIP DRY·

The very fabric of space is deformed by the presence of a black hole, drawing everything in.

Once within the "event horizon" of a black hole, nothing can escape.

ARTIST'S CONCEPTION OF THE INTERIOR OF A BLACK HOLE
Theories suggest it may also contain campaign promises, missing Watergate tapes, and Jimmy Hoffa. ▼

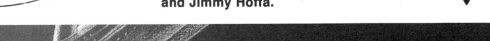

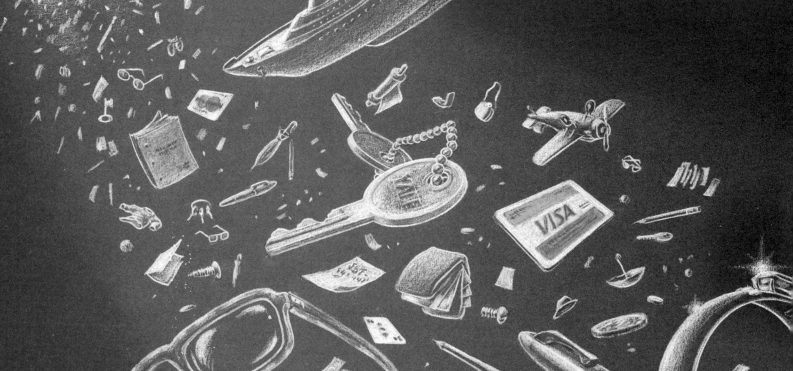

The Solar System

Many theories had to be tried and discarded before our present understanding of the solar system was achieved. Some primitive peoples, for example, believed that the world was supported on the back of a tortoise, which in turn rode on the back of an elephant, which in turn rode in the back of a '56 Chevy Bel Air.

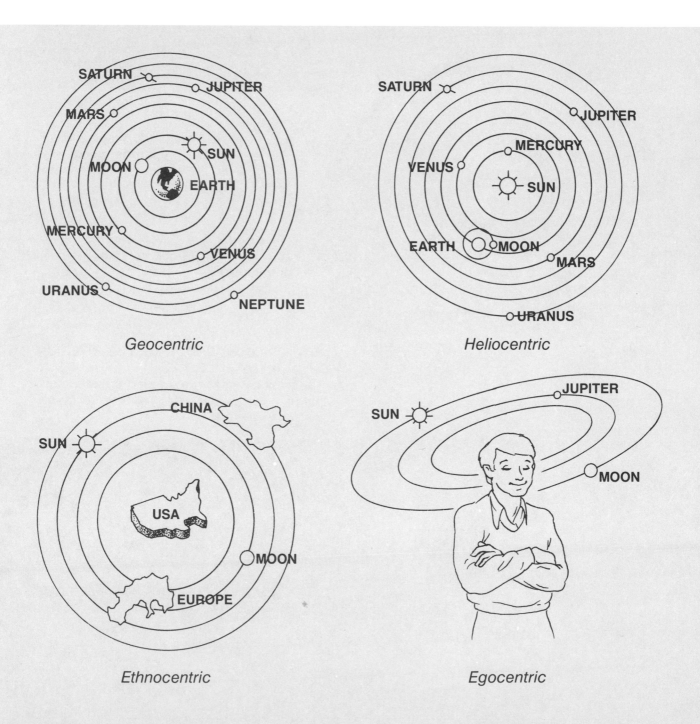

Geocentric

Heliocentric

Ethnocentric

Egocentric

Today we recognize that there are nine planets, each revolving around the sun.

To understand the relative scale of the solar system, imagine that the earth is a tennis ball and is located in the middle of Times Square. Venus, to the same scale, would be a golf ball in Buffalo. Likewise, Mercury would be a badminton bird in Pontiac, Michigan, and Mars a hockey puck in Calumet City, Illinois.

The sun would be the size of the Hyatt-Regency Hotel in Fort Lauderdale, Florida. Jupiter would be the same size and location as the average Central American right-wing dictator; and Saturn would be a rabid Doberman in Anaheim, California.

Uranus would be a Cranshaw melon imported at great expense to Moosejaw, Saskatchewan; Neptune, a typical serving of french fries in Pocatello, Idaho; and Pluto, an excellent Pont-L'Evêque cheese in a charming little bistro in Paris.

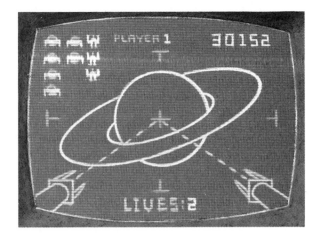

Image of Saturn returned by the Atari-12 video probe.

Planets of the Solar System				
Name	**Symbol**	**Satellites**	**Atmosphere**	**Life**
MERCURY	🌡	0	None	No
VENUS		0	Corrosive	No
EARTH		Classified	Smoggy	Yes
MARS		2	Thin	Invisible
JUPITER		16	Thick	Cute, big blue eyes
SATURN		17	Casual	Only on Saturday night
URANUS		5	Quaint	Published monthly these days
NEPTUNE		2	Continental	Yes, if you call this living
PLUTO		0	None, but the food is great	Just a bowl of cherries

Jupiter viewed through a whiskey glass in a cocktail lounge on Callisto.

Saturn's rings, looking over the shoulder of a gerbil blown out of a volcano on Titan.

Artist's Conceptions of the Planets

World-famous space artist Paracelsus Barley precisely calculated the spatial relationships of the moons and planets in order to achieve scientific accuracy in these paintings.

Reflection of three-quarters-full Neptune in a lake of liquid sulphur on Triton as seen while hanging upside-down from parallel bars.

THE REALITY
This Viking lander photograph shows Mars' two moons, Verbose and Des Moines, over a barren, lifeless Martian landscape.

Sun, Moon, and Earth

The sun and the moon are the two most important heavenly bodies in our daily lives.

The sun is the source of all earth's energy. This is important because one day we're going to get the bill.

The surface of the sun sometimes erupts into giant bursts of flame, or **solar flares,** which can disrupt radio and TV communication on earth. This is yet another of the sun's beneficial effects.

Blemishes called **sunspots** also mar the sun's face. Sunspots appear and disappear

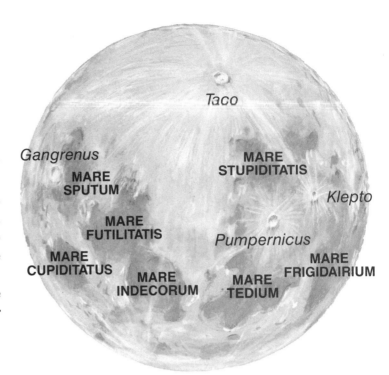

Taco

Gangrenus

MARE SPUTUM

MARE STUPIDITATIS

Klepto

MARE FUTILITATIS

Pumpernicus

MARE CUPIDITATUS

MARE INDECORUM

MARE TEDIUM

MARE FRIGIDAIRIUM

SUNSPOTS IN BENIGN PHASE
Stock market up, Republicans in, miniskirt back.

in a complex regular cycle. Statistical analyses of these cycles have shown them to be significantly related to stock market fluctuations, presidential elections, and skirt lengths.

The moon is our nearest neighbor in space. Its cold, airless surface is covered with craters and broad seas called **maria.** This is the origin of the popular lunar song, "They Call the Maria Wind."

Ask Dr. Stupid

What Holds the Moon Up?

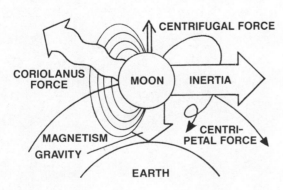

CENTRIFUGAL FORCE

CORIOLANUS FORCE

MOON

INERTIA

MAGNETISM

GRAVITY

CENTRI-PETAL FORCE

EARTH

The moon can't fall down because it is in **orbit.** An orbit is the interaction of a combination of forces—such as gravity, inertia, centrifugal force, and others—that result in a perfect balance.

Nevertheless, it is a good idea to stay indoors as much as possible.

Eclipses

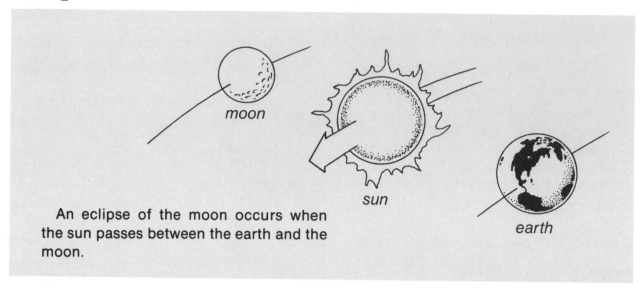

An eclipse of the moon occurs when the sun passes between the earth and the moon.

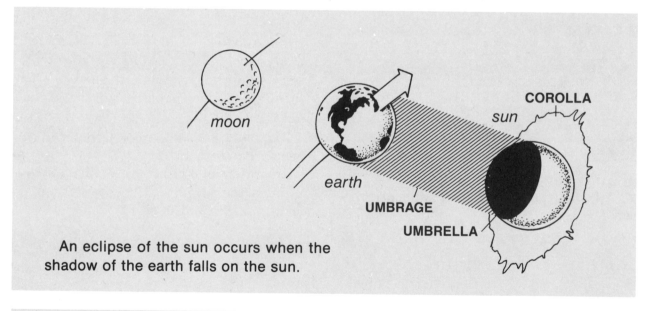

An eclipse of the sun occurs when the shadow of the earth falls on the sun.

An eclipse of the earth occurs when you put your hands over your eyes.

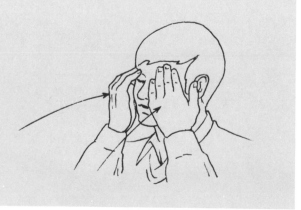

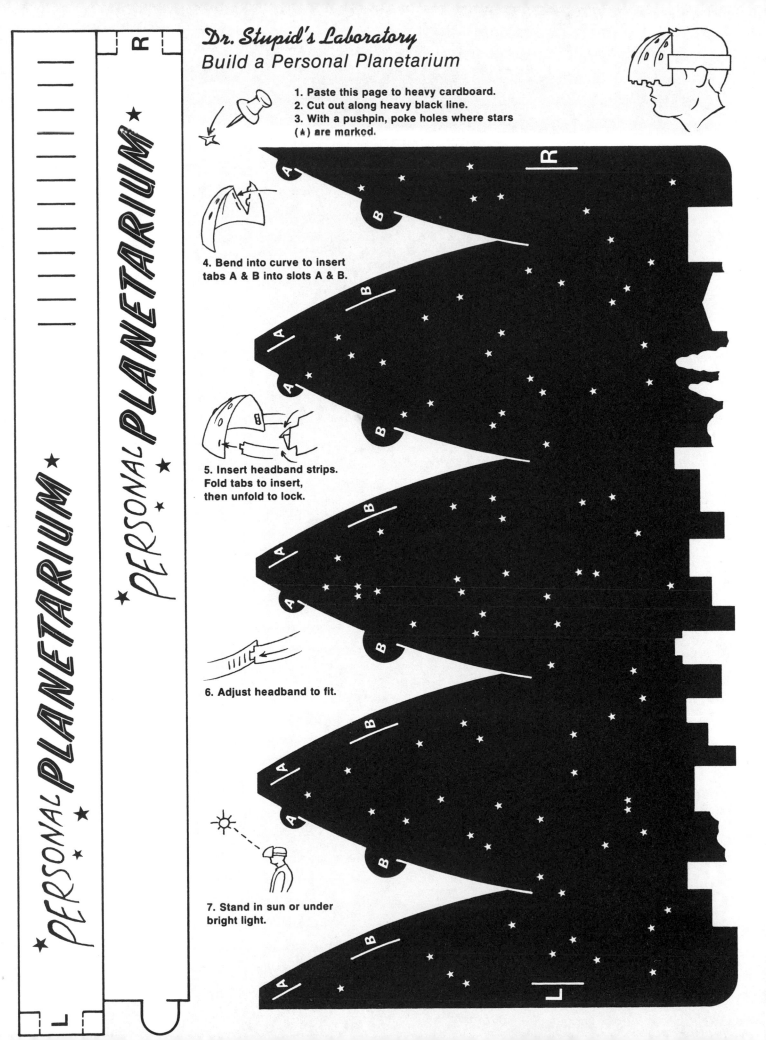

Dr. Stupid's Laboratory
Build a Personal Planetarium

1. Paste this page to heavy cardboard.
2. Cut out along heavy black line.
3. With a pushpin, poke holes where stars (★) are marked.

4. Bend into curve to insert tabs A & B into slots A & B.

5. Insert headband strips. Fold tabs to insert, then unfold to lock.

6. Adjust headband to fit.

7. Stand in sun or under bright light.

PERSONAL PLANETARIUM

PERSONAL PLANETARIUM

2. Matter and Energy

Man's first application of the laws governing matter and energy was his invention of the **basic machines.** This was a great step forward for civilization; but it involved only an intuitive understanding of mechanics. An explanation of the underlying principles came with the rise of experimental science.

Galileo and Gravity

Galileo's demonstration of the laws of gravity is a perfect example of the use of the scientific method. For a thousand years before Galileo, people had accepted the theory of gravity propounded by Aristotle.

Aristotle alleged that heavy and light

Basic Machines

Early man had to rely on his muscles alone in his daily work. With the advance of civilization, the burden was lightened by the discovery of these labor-saving devices.

THE LOAFER

Force exerted by load raises end of lever to convenient height for resting.

THE DISINCLINED PLANE

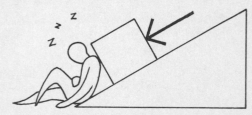

Downward force of load provides support to lean against.

THE FLAT TIRE

Useless wheel prevents moving load; might as well take a nap.

THE BLOCKED TACKLE

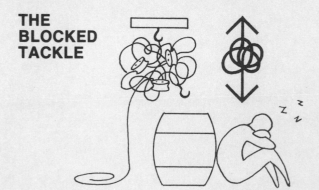

As ropes are hopelessly tangled, the load cannot be lifted.

THE SCREWUP

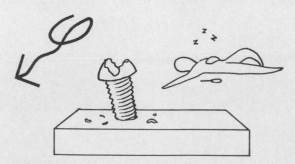

After ruining the screw, the job might as well be given up.

Thus, the Law of Conservation of Energy is demonstrated.

objects fell at the same rate. To explain the obvious exceptions, he invoked an ideal state he called a "vacuum." Only in this imaginary and purely theoretical state could the "true" behavior of falling objects be observed.

Galileo overturned this idealized theory in a famous experiment. He dropped a feather and a lead weight from the top of the Leaning Tower of Pisa. The feather drifted down slowly, while the lead weight plummeted quickly. Thus, by the use of the experimental method, Galileo showed that heavy objects fall faster than light ones.

Newton's Laws

Isaac Newton also used direct observation to formulate his laws. Newton was in government service for many years. His First Law states:

A body at rest tends to remain at rest, while a body in motion at a constant velocity in a straight line tends to continue in that motion.

Clearly, this law is based on firsthand observation of a bureaucracy in action.

Once Newton became engaged in a heated argument in a bar over the question of epicycles, leading him to punch his opponent in the nose. After contemplating the results, he announced his law:

Every action has an equal and opposite reaction.

In the famous story, Newton discovered gravity when he was hit on the head while sitting under an apple tree. This tale is fictitious, of course. It was actually a fig tree, resulting in his best-known theory:

I'll bet you could make a swell cookie out of figs.

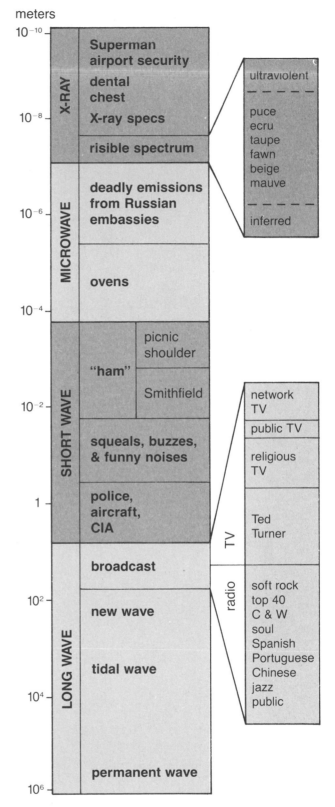

**THE ELECTROMAGNETIC SPECTRUM
All heated bodies emit radiation in the form of waves. The type of radiation depends on the length of the wave.**

Periodic Table of the Elements

Group headers (left to right): 1A · 2B · NOT 2B · 3D · 4F · A · B-C · D-H · I-M · N-W · X-Y-Z · Other · R2-D2

Main table

1A	2B	NOT 2B	3D	4F	R2-D2
Li LINT 1					Sc SCUM 2
De DENIM 3	To TOFU 4			Hy HYDROX 5	Cl CLOROX 6
Ny NYLON 7	Je JELL-O 8	Al ALIMONY 9	Ph PHLEGM 10	Ch CHOCOLATE 11	Wd WD-40 12
Te TEFLON 13	Ve VELVEETA 14	Feh IRONY 15	Me MENTHOLATUM 16	Bi BISMARCK 17	Dr DRANO 18
Ve VELCRO 19	Mz MARZIPAN 20	Ar ARGOT 21	Ln LANOLIN 22	Ga GARLIC 23	Lm LINOLEUM 24
Xe XEROX 25*	Pa PASTA 30	Po POLONIUS 31	Pr PRELL 32	Zi ZINFANDEL 33	Ma MASONITE 34
Ko KODACHROME 35†	Gr GRANOLA 40	Pd PANDEMONIUM 41	Lb LIBRIUM 42		

Special series

A	B-C	D-H	I-M
Fl FLIT 26	Ra RAID 27	Bu BUGGETA 28	St STEPONUM 29
Kr KRYPTONITE 36	Di DILITHIUM 37	Ca CAVORITE 38	La LAETRILE 39

*Insecticides

†Fantasides

The Elements

The early alchemists thought that there were only four kinds of matter, or **elements**—earth, air, fire, and water.

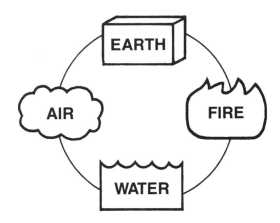

All the different kinds of matter we see around us were believed to come from mixtures of these four. While this was a good start, four elements alone did not seem to provide enough diversity to account for all matter.

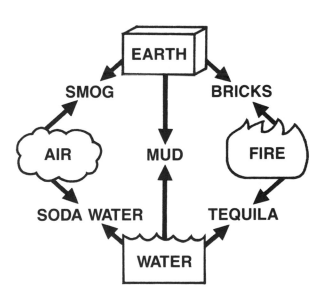

Today we recognize far more elements than the ancients, and can arrange them in a **periodic table** (left) to make them appear impressive and hard to understand.

The Atom

The elements are made up of still more basic bits of matter called **atoms.**

Democritus' atom

The earliest theories held that the atom was hard, round, and indivisible, like a dormitory meatball.

Rutherford's atom

In the twentieth century it was discovered that atoms consisted of three smaller particles. This was still tolerable and made a nice graphic symbol for corporate logos.

modern atom

Today, things have gone seriously downhill. Our modern picture of the atom has little lines zinging off (to represent the hundreds of subatomic particles that have been discovered), and is represented as a blur (on account of Heisenberg's Uncertainty Principle, which says that you can't tell where anything is).*

---

*A fuller discussion of Heisenberg's Uncertainty Principle may be found in the Appendix. Then again, it may not.

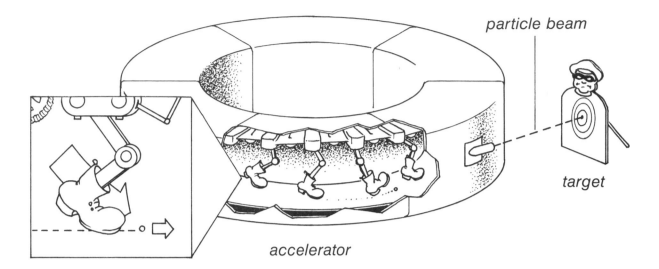

particle beam

target

accelerator

Splitting the Atom

You may wish to skip over the following discussion—and any other discussion of the subject you encounter in the next several years, until you hear that the whole thing has gotten sorted out.

The decline of modern physics began with the **particle accelerator.** The particle accelerator is a device that turns your taxes into a small beam of subatomic particles.

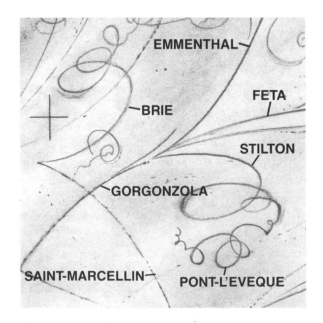

EMMENTHAL

BRIE

FETA

STILTON

GORGONZOLA

SAINT-MARCELLIN

PONT-L'EVEQUE

cheese-chamber photograph

The particles are initially generated by dumping several billion dollars into a Cuisinart equipped with the extra-fine blade. Placed in the accelerator, the particles are given small "kicks" as they move around a track. Each successive kick adds to their speed, so that they whirl faster and faster.

Of course, as Einstein tells us, there is an upper limit on speed, faster than which nothing is permitted to travel.* Having reached this maximum velocity, the particles emerge in a beam, which is directed at a target.

At the target, the beam collides with an atom, causing its constituent particles to fly apart. The particles themselves are invisible; but their "tracks" can be detected using devices such as the cloud chamber, the bubble chamber, or the **cheese chamber.**

The cheese chamber holds a solution of milk curd under precisely controlled pre-cheese conditions. The particle passing through the solution causes it to coagulate, leaving a track of cheese. The types of particles released can be determined from the types of cheese produced.

*55 miles per hour.

The proliferation of particles (right) has led to an attempt to simplify the system. Thus it is theorized that they are all made up of a single particle with various properties, called a **quack** (and its anti-particle, the **quirk**). Shown below are the currently understood properties of the quack.

An amusing though less plausible parody of this material can be found in any book on current particle physics.

	particle	anti-particle
HADRIANS	BARONS neutron proton bo's'on	BORONS neutroff protoff bo's'on's mate
	MASONS mu stigma phi beta kappa	DIXONS nu? smegma abba dabba
TEUTONS	torino eclectron	steverino exxon

Some of the more popular subatomic particles.

	straight up		on the rocks	
posture **credit rating** **MPG** **starch**	red rich play atchison	white middle-class record topeka	rosé poor rewind santa fe	**raw**
posture **credit rating** **MPG** **starch**	groucho filter two-door haystack	harpo menthol four-door december	chico king-size hatchback 1776	**cooked**
	weekdays	**Sundays & holidays**		

The First Nuclear Reactor

The Manhattan Project, which created the first sustained nuclear reaction, was one of two top-secret World War II experiments. Through a clerical error, it was inadvertently located in Chicago.

Its sister program, the Chicago Project (headquartered in Manhattan), was originally thought the more promising. The goal was a machine that would convert electrical energy into U^{235}. Dropped on German cities, it would cripple the Nazi war machine by absorbing the electrical power from war plants and communications, and further create confusion by blocking roads with the heaps of uranium it produced.

To everyone's surprise, it was the Manhattan group that succeeded, creating a device that could generate power from the breakdown of uranium. The competing Chicago Project is now only a footnote to History.*

*History, footnote, p. 563.

Relativity

The principles of relativity are too well known today to require explanation. The humblest reader of this book can undoubtedly give a clear and concise account of such relativistic phenomena as the Michelson-Morley experiment, the Lorentz-Fitzgerald contraction, and the Dow-Jones average. The familiar **world-line diagram** sums it all up:

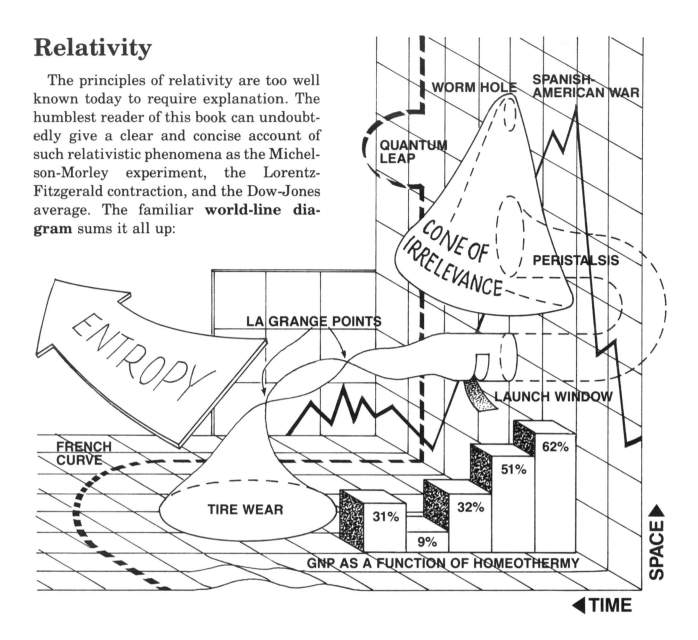

Now that your memory is refreshed, try testing your wits on this simple problem in relativity:

You are the pilot of an interstellar spaceship traveling from Earth to Alpha Centauri. On leaving Earth, the spaceship accelerates continuously until it reaches the midpoint of its journey, at which point it is traveling at 7/8 the speed of light. It then decelerates at an equivalent rate for the remainder of the trip. Simultaneously with its departure, a radio signal is sent from Alpha Centauri to Earth, traveling (of course) at the speed of light. When the ship arrives at Alpha Centauri, a clock on board shows that five months have elapsed during the trip. To an observer on Earth, the radio signal appears to have arrived 4.2 years after the ship's departure.

Problem: What is the name of the pilot's mother?

Dr. Stupid's Laboratory
Build a Nuclear Reactor

A back-yard nuclear reactor is easy to build, and a fascinating educational project. It can also produce an inexpensive supply of hot water—handy in these days of high fuel bills! Just follow these step-by-step instructions.

You will need:
- A 32-gallon plastic trash can (heavy-duty, and preferably with locking handles to discourage inquisitive pets and children)
- 45 feet of 3″ PVC plumbing pipe
- 10 feet of 2½″ PVC plumbing pipe
- A keyhole saw
- A hacksaw
- Duct tape
- A meat thermometer
- 12 standard 75 mm rods of U^{235}*

1. Cut your three-inch piping into 28″ lengths—nineteen in all. Position the sections vertically in the trash can as shown. A few inches of sand in the bottom will help hold them if necessary.

2. With the keyhole saw, cut seven holes in the trash can lid, corresponding to the locations of the pipes in the diagram (color). These are for inserting your control rods. Cut three more smaller holes as shown.

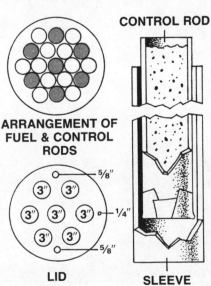

ARRANGEMENT OF FUEL & CONTROL RODS

5/8″ 1/4″ 5/8″

3″ 3″ 3″ 3″ 3″ 3″ 3″

LID

CONTROL ROD

SLEEVE

3. Now for the control rods. Cut the smaller pipe into 34″ lengths—seven in all. Seal one end securely with duct tape. Fill each rod to the top with an appropriate damping material. The "pros" use graphite, but a good potting soil will work nicely.

4. Slide the fuel rods into the correct pipes, following the diagram. Safety first! Wear gardening gloves when handling the U^{235}.

5. Pop on the lid, lining up the holes with the control rod sleeves. Insert a garden hose in one of the 5/8″ holes, and fill the trash can right to the top. Heavy water is best here. (If you live near a nuclear power plant, you may already be getting heavy water from your tap. If not, plain water will do.)

A second garden hose will carry the heated water out, provided the can is higher than the end of the hose. **NOTE: Before doing steps 4 & 5, be sure to insert the control rods into their sleeves. Otherwise, there is the risk of a "runaway" reaction.** The inserted rods will stick up six inches above the lid, so you can grasp them for removal.

6. Push the meat thermometer into the small hole in the lid. Now, by altering the flow of water from the faucet, and by removing more or fewer control rods, you should be able to maintain a constant temperature inside the reactor.

You can use the hot water you produce to run a toy turbine, heat your doghouse, or fill a hot tub. Any overflow can irrigate your garden, where it will often produce beautiful and unusual foliage. Always dispose of spent fuel rods properly.

*U^{235} rods can often be obtained through local hobby or terrorist groups. Or order by mail from Bud's Scientific Supply, 1113 E. 7th St., Slagheap, NJ 08865. You must state that you are over twenty-one.

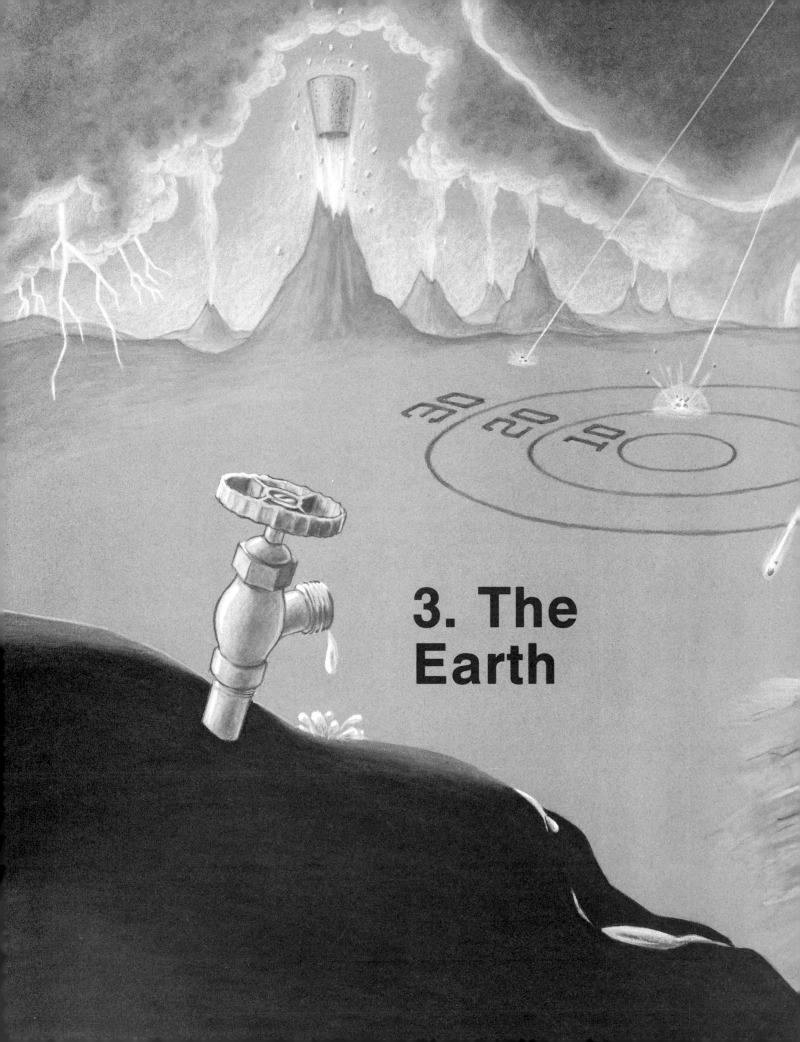

3. The Earth

The Interior of the Earth

The earth is covered by a light, flaky outer layer called the **crust**. The heavier inner part is called the **filling**. It is made up mostly of molten rock, or **magda**.

The upper part of the filling is called the **mantle**. Below that is the hot center, or **fireplace**.

The composition of the earth's center is thought to be primarily iron, with about 5% nickel and 10% dime, and traces of niacin and riboflavin.

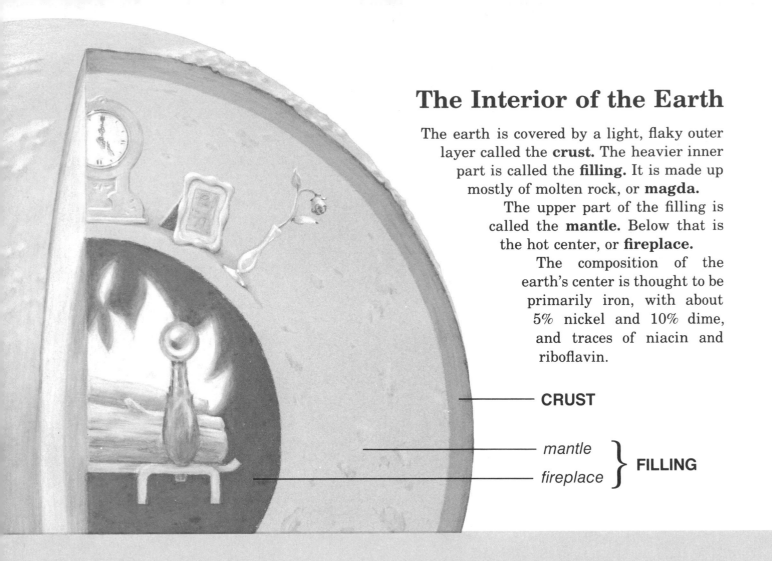

CRUST

mantle
fireplace } **FILLING**

Types of Rocks

Rocks are classified into three types according to whether they come from volcanic magda, sediments deposited on the ocean floor, or your shoe.

appearance			
type	IGNOMINIOUS	SEDENTARY	METAPHORIC
examples	grabit	flent	scheiss
	feldman	cherk	gnash
	quarts	snale	slake
	hornswoggle	slimestone	hornrim
	appetite	sodomite	garnish
	olivetti	limonade	marvel
	garbo	travestine	anthrocide

Tides

We sometimes speak of tides causing the oceans to rise or fall. Of course, this is a fallacy. Actually, it is the *land* that rises and falls.

As the earth rotates, the moon's gravitational attraction is greatest first on one side, then the other. Land masses, being rigid, are pulled up or down accordingly. Oceans, being liquid, are free to flow back to their normal level.

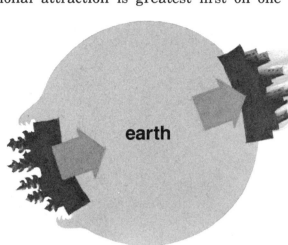

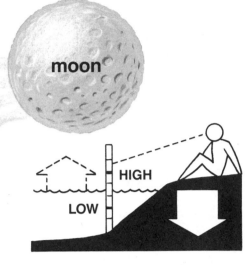

To observer, water level appears to rise; actually, land has sunk.

Volcanoes

Volcanic eruptions are caused either by a buildup of pressure on subterranean pockets of molten rock, or by angering the gods. The eruption generally continues until the crater is plugged by solidifying lava or virgins.

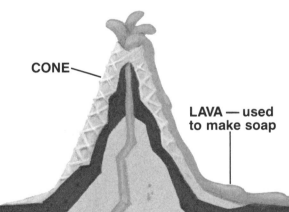

CONE

LAVA — used to make soap

MOLTEN MAGDA

Ask Dr. Stupid

Why is the sky blue?

Because it reflects the sea.

Continental Drift

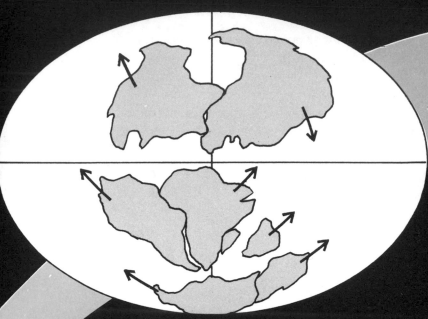

2.

By the end of the Styptic era, continental drift has split Pangaea into two super-continents on either side of the 20th parallel—Laurasia to the north and Gondwana to the south.

1.

Around 200 million years ago, the continents are jammed together in a single great land mass called Pangaea.

Plate Tectonics

The surface of the earth is made up of independently moving sections called **plates.** Their motion—sliding, grinding, and colliding with one another—gives rise to the phenomenon of **continental drift.**

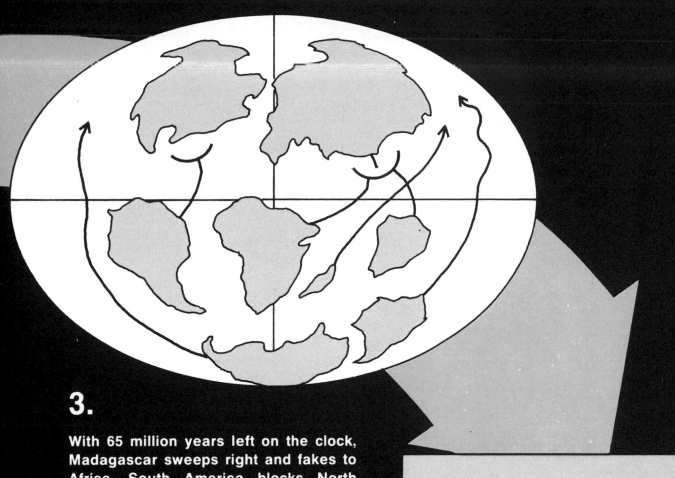

3.

With 65 million years left on the clock, Madagascar sweeps right and fakes to Africa. South America blocks North America's rush. Australia goes wide as Antarctica runs a post pattern downfield. Eurasia reads the play but is hooked in by a block from the Indian subcontinent.

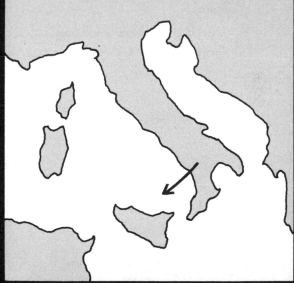

4.

The current phase of continental drift begins. Situation calls for an onside kick.

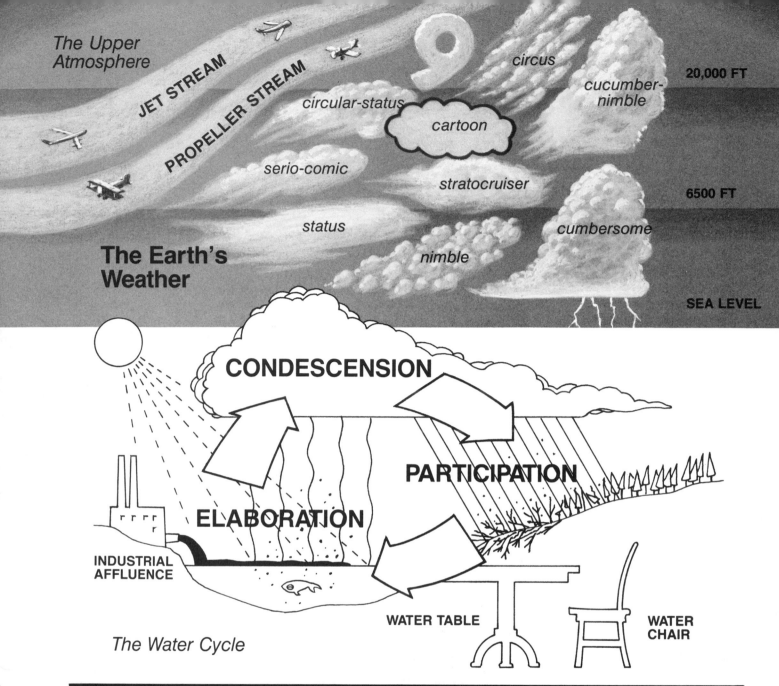

The Upper Atmosphere

JET STREAM

PROPELLER STREAM

circular-status

circus

cucumber-nimble — 20,000 FT

cartoon

serio-comic

stratocruiser

6500 FT

status

cumbersome

The Earth's Weather

nimble

SEA LEVEL

CONDESCENSION

PARTICIPATION

ELABORATION

INDUSTRIAL AFFLUENCE

WATER TABLE

WATER CHAIR

The Water Cycle

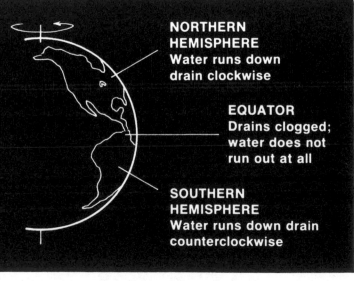

The Coriolanus Effect

Since the earth is a rotating sphere, different points on its surface move at different velocities depending on their platitude. The result of this unequal velocity—the **Coriolanus effect**—causes storm systems to rotate clockwise north of the equator and counterclockwise to the south. This effect even influences which way water in a sink will swirl as it runs down the drain.

NORTHERN HEMISPHERE
Water runs down drain clockwise

EQUATOR
Drains clogged; water does not run out at all

SOUTHERN HEMISPHERE
Water runs down drain counterclockwise

How to Read a Weather Map

Weather maps often appear in the papers or on TV. If you know how to apply the key, you can interpret their meaning in everyday language.

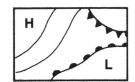

"Looks like rain. Or mebbe not."

"Might be a big 'un. Less'n it clears up."

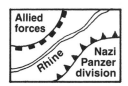

"Dunno. Hard to say, I reckon."

"Sure are in for a spell o' weather. Yup."

Testing Rain for Probability

You've probably heard the weatherman predict a "30% chance" or a "70% probability" of rain. You can check the chance of rain having fallen for yourself with a back-yard **rain probability gauge.**

Let's say it rained during the night. What were the chances of that rain occurring?
1. Check the gauge—which is marked in inches just like a regular rain gauge—for the level of rainwater, and mark it down. This represents the level of actual rainfall (which will always be the same as the level of probable rainfall).
2. Next, check the level of nonprobable rainfall (which you can also think of as probable nonrainfall). Since nonprobable rain is lighter than probable rain, the nonrain will float on top of the rainwater.

Probabilities, of course, are invisible. To render them measurable, the rain probability gauge contains a probability float to mark the level of nonprobable rain. A probability float can be made of any material less probable than rain, and hence lighter. Except in very dry parts of the world, this presents no problem; an entry stub from the Publishers

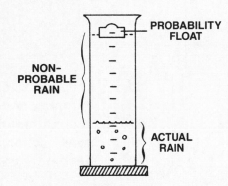

Clearing House Sweepstakes will do nicely. Alternatively, a few drops of statistician's ink can be added to the column to make it visible.

3. To the two levels, apply the formula

$$\frac{\text{actual rain}}{\text{total probable \& nonprobable rain}} = \% \text{ chance}$$

In the illustration, 3″ of rain divided by 10″ of nonrain gives .30, telling you that the three inches of rain that fell did so as a result of a 30% chance of rain.

If it has not rained, and the gauge is dry, proceed as follows:
1. Mark down the level of the probability float.
2. From a watering can or garden hose, slowly add water to the column until the probability float starts to rise.

This approach is based on the fact that the bottom of the gauge contains a certain level of probable rain, just as before, but without any actual water to make it visible. Since real rain must contain equal volumes of water and the probability of water, the probability in the bottom of the column will absorb just its own volume of the water you add, and no more.

3. Measure the level of water and the new level of the float.
4. Subtract from the water level a volume of water equal to the rise in the probability float, as this represents water in excess of the probability level.
5. Divide this figure by the total capacity of the gauge, thus deriving the odds from which your dry spell resulted.

Earthquakes: Whose Fault?

1 Earthquake prediction appears in press.

2 Alarmed public starts "earthquake-proofing" homes, buildings.

3 Birds and animals, sensing fear among humans, and upset by commotion of increased construction work, become agitated.

5 Earthquake occurs.

4 Vibration from construction and from animals jumping up and down on surface is transmitted to fault.

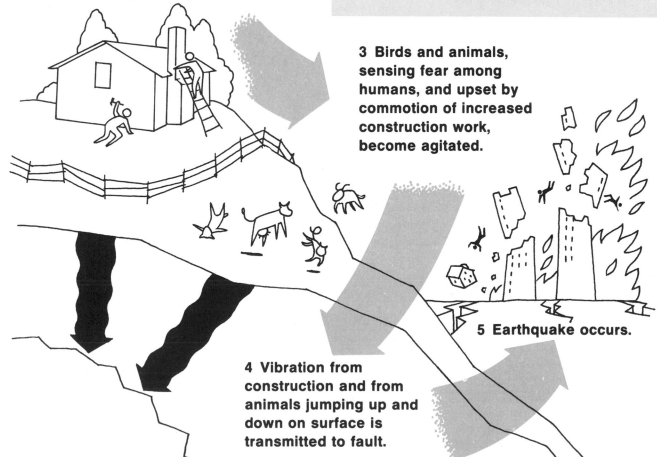

Dr. Stupid's Laboratory: Build a Seismometer

1. Paste this page to heavy cardboard.
2. Cut out along heavy black line.

seismOmeter

ASSEMBLED INSTRUMENT

7.5

6.5

5

3

PASSING TRUCK

MILD QUAKE or party upstairs

MEDIUM QUAKE or swell party upstairs

STRONG QUAKE or nearby small children

DEVASTATING QUAKE or your water heater exploding

A

B

A A

B B

TOP

HOOK

A

B

C

D

A

3. To assemble pointer:
   a. Fold hook down.
   b. Fold up along all other dotted lines.
   c. Tuck flap D under top of pointer.
   d. Insert tabs A, B, & C into slots A, B, & C.

4. To assemble base:
   a. Fold up along all dotted lines.
   b. Insert tabs A & B into slots A & B.
5. Hang pointer from hole at top of base.

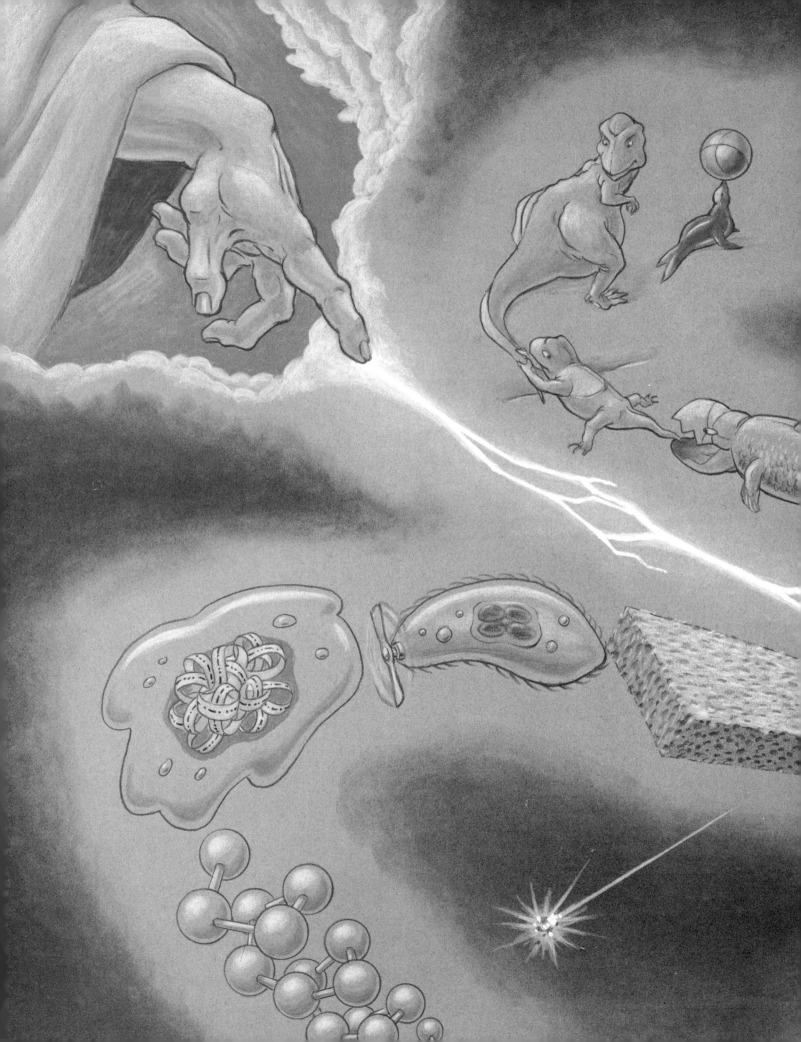

4. Evolution

How Do We Know About Ancient Creatures?

Scientists who study the extinct creatures that once roamed the earth are called **paleontologists.** If you were to watch a paleontologist at work, you would probably see him on his hands and knees, methodically and painstakingly examining the surface of the ground. This is because he is looking for **fossils,** or else has lost a contact lens.

A fossil is any trace left behind by a living thing. Usually the term refers to mineralized bones, but it can also include teeth, eggs, footprints, and unpaid phone bills.

By careful analysis, paleontologists can often reconstruct a whole animal from just a tiny fragment of bone.

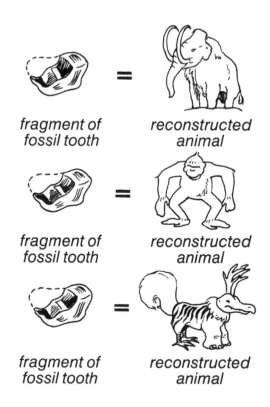

fragment of
fossil tooth

reconstructed
animal

fragment of
fossil tooth

reconstructed
animal

fragment of
fossil tooth

reconstructed
animal

By collecting and analyzing fossils, paleontologists have succeeded in tracing the entire history of life on earth, from the first living things to modern man. Of course, there are tiny gaps in the record, and minor uncertainties of interpretation. Nevertheless, the overall picture is clearly understood.

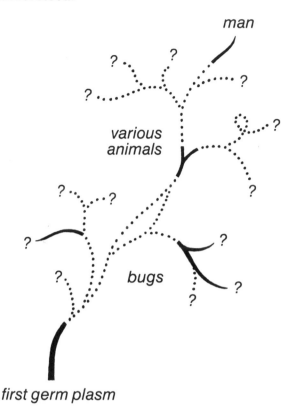

man

various
animals

bugs

first germ plasm

How Does Evolution Work?

Animals of a given species are alike because they inherit a certain set of genes from their parents. Every so often, something goes wrong with the mechanism that transmits the genes, and an animal is born that doesn't resemble its father and mother. You probably know of examples in your own family.

If this accidental variation, or **mutation,** is helpful in the animal's struggle to survive, it is more likely to be passed on to succeeding generations. In this way, new species can arise.

There are different theories about exactly how this works. According to the **gradualist** theory, the accumulation of tiny changes over thousands of years finally results in an entirely new animal.

gradualism

0   10,000 years   20,000 years   30,000 years

Those who favor evolution by **saltation** believe that species can arise by sudden "jumps," under the pressure of an altered environment.

saltation

0   2 seconds   4 seconds   6 seconds

Finally, there is a combination of the two, known as **punctuated equilibrium.**

punctuated equilibrium

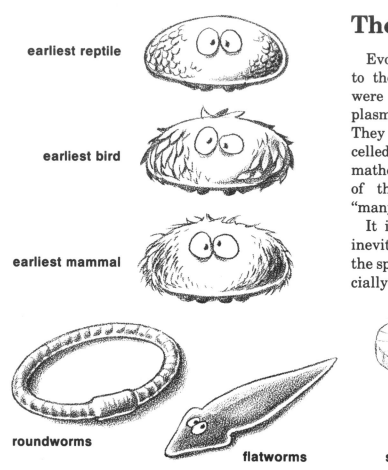

earliest reptile

earliest bird

earliest mammal

The First Living Things

Evolution proceeds from simpler forms to the more complex. The first animals were simple one-celled blobs of protoplasm. Then two-celled animals arose. They were followed by three-celled, four-celled, five-celled, etc. (If you find the mathematics here too difficult, just think of the numbers larger than one as "many.")

It is easy to see how this process led inevitably to more complex forms such as the sponges, the worms, and so forth. Especially if you don't think about it too much.

roundworms

flatworms

squareworms

triangularworms

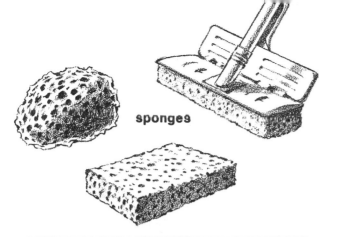

sponges

GRAPHITES
Among the earliest fossil records, the graphites resemble pencil marks on the rock formations they occur in.

~~FORMANIFRIA~~
~~FOMINORFIA~~
~~FAMOR~~
SEASHELLS
These microscopic one-celled animals bore shells in an amazing variety of shapes.

THE ORTHOPEDIC OCEAN
Shells were so successful as a defense that a wide range of shelled life evolved. The Orthopedic sea floor must have been an eerie scene, its perpetual silence broken only by the incessant chanting of the mantra ray.

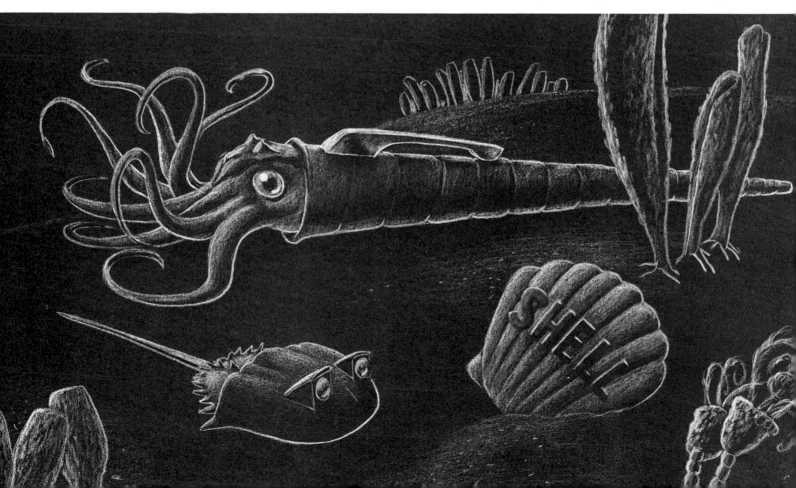

A remarkable example of a "living fossil" is the primitive ~~caleocanth~~ ~~celoacanth~~ ~~ceola~~ **this ugly sucker here.** Thought to have been extinct for millions of years, it was rediscovered when a paleontologist was served a poorly preserved but recognizable specimen in a world-famous seafood restaurant. The paleontologist was naturally astonished, as he had ordered the red snapper.

Conquest of the Land—The Amphibians

The first vertebrates to exploit the rich food resources of the land were the **amphibians** (from the Greek *amphi-*, slimy + *bios*, dumb). Many species attempted the transition without success. These early forms were hampered by their limited range and mobility on land.

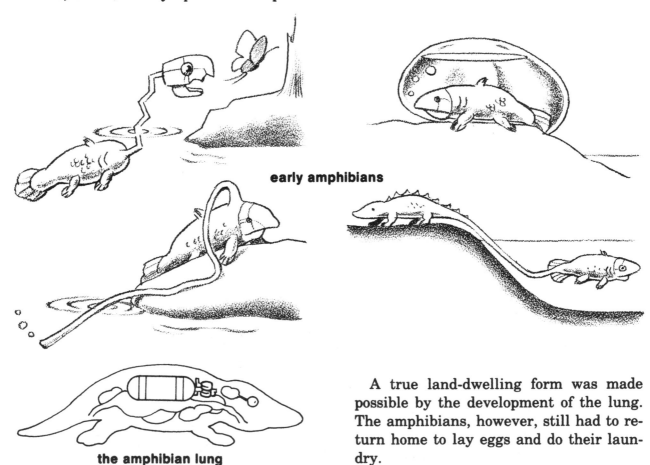

early amphibians

the amphibian lung

A true land-dwelling form was made possible by the development of the lung. The amphibians, however, still had to return home to lay eggs and do their laundry.

46

Puppisaurus

woolly turtle

Bovidon

The Mammal-like Reptiles

This group, with characteristics that foreshadowed those of the later mammals, arose early in the development of the reptiles. However, other reptilian orders became the dominant terrestrial forms, crowding out these forward-looking species. As you may have noticed, often when you arise too early, you're no good for the rest of the day.

armored mammoth

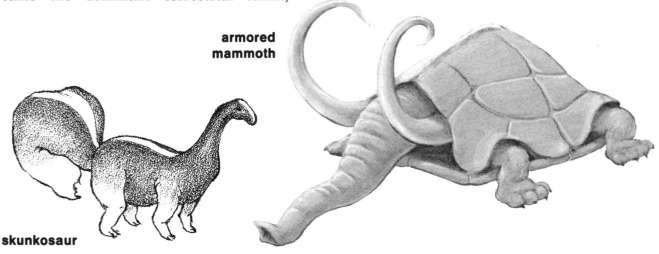

skunkosaur

a fern or something

The Plant Kingdom

The evolution of plants is an important chapter in the history of life. However, it's a pretty dull chapter, so we'll skip it.

The Age of Dinosaurs

The reptiles reached their peak with the rise of the dinosaurs (from the Greek *dino,* ugly + *sauros,* smells bad).

For millions of years the earth trembled under the footsteps of these giant reptiles, such as the fierce *Tyrannosaurus rex* (opposite). This reconstruction reflects the current view that the dinosaurs, for all their size and ferocity, may have been closely related to birds.

At the end of the Metatarsal, the dinosaurs abruptly vanished. The theory that a single catastrophic event may have been responsible has been strengthened by the recent discovery of a worldwide layer of whipped cream marking the Creosote-Tutelary boundary.

Thesaurus

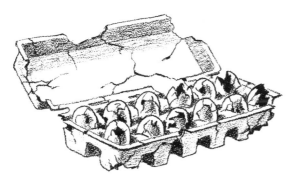

Dinosaur eggs, found remarkably preserved at Devil's Food Processor National Monument, Wyoming.

Some experts have questioned this restoration of these unusual saurians, as fossil remains of the two species are invariably found in association.

Diplocephalus

Diplocaudus

pelicosaur

Reptiles of the Sea and Air

The reptiles at their peak filled all the available ecological niches. Some returned to the sea, while others took to the air.

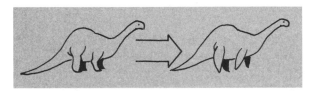

The evolutionary process that produced the aquatic dinosaurs is easy to visualize. The transformation of the feet into flippers adapted them perfectly to life in the seas. Being reptiles, of course, they still had to return to the land to lay eggs and attend class reunions.

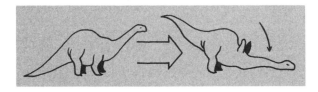

The development of flight presents a more difficult problem of adaptation.

Clearly any intermediate stage in the transformation of both front legs into wings would create problems, such as falling over forward. Instead, forms such as *Monopterasaurus* developed. Though a fierce carnivore, it could only fly in circles. Perhaps it inhabited the dense Metatarsal forests, where it could effectively pursue its prey around tree trunks.

Monopterosaurus

This is what these creatures would look like as outlines with numbers on them.

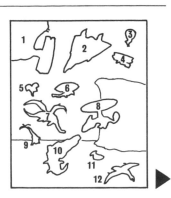

Life in the Metatarsal

Paint-by-Number
1. dark green
2. yellow
3. red ochre
4. burnt umber
5. crimson
6. dark brown
7. green
8. light blue
9. light green
10. blue-green

old view of dinosaurs

The dinosaurs have traditionally been pictured as slow, stupid, and lethargic beasts. Recent thinking suggests that they may in fact have been intelligent, active, and well-adapted to their environment.

new view of dinosaurs

Footprints in the Sands of Time

These dinosaur tracks, from Devil's Hot Tub State Park, Wyoming, suggest an unknown species with a specialized mode of locomotion.

Scientists have reconstructed this dinosaur on the basis of a track found at Devil's Tax Shelter National Monument, Wyoming.

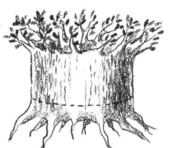

This pattern led to the identification of the shortest known giant redwood—*Sequoia brevis.* Extrapolating from the size of the animal track, the dwarf redwood stood only sixteen inches tall. (From Devil's Torque Wrench Wilderness Area, Wyoming.)

This track suggests that some species may have rebelled against the incessant conflict that marked the Creosote Era in what is now Devil's Three-Martini Lunch National Forest, Wyoming.

Ask Dr. Stupid

Why Did the Dinosaurs Die Out?

(pick one)

- ☐ Climate got colder
- ☐ Drought
- ☐ Flood
- ☐ Became too numerous
- ☐ Became too scarce
- ☐ Glaciers
- ☐ Eggs eaten by small mammals
- ☐ Toes eaten by small mammals
- ☐ Constipation
- ☐ Racial old age
- ☐ Fell in tar pits

- ☐ Too big
- ☐ Too dumb
- ☐ Too ugly
- ☐ Volcanoes
- ☐ Earth struck by asteroid
- ☐ Earth struck by comet
- ☐ Earth struck by whipped-cream pie
- ☐ Warts
- ☐ Herpes
- ☐ Lead in water supply
- ☐ Rising expectations

This list may also be used to explain the fall of the Roman Empire, the French Revolution, and World War I.

**saber-toothed
duck**

The Birds

At the end of the Creosote, two new classes arose to challenge the ruling reptiles—birds and mammals.

The birds' success was due in large part to their development of the feather. As you may recall from chapter 2, Galileo demonstrated that a feather falls more slowly than a lead weight. Being covered with feathers thus gave the birds a definite advantage over the flying reptiles, which were covered with lead weights.

Other flying forms appeared during this period, many of which proved unsuccessful.

Gigantopsittacus, largest of the avians

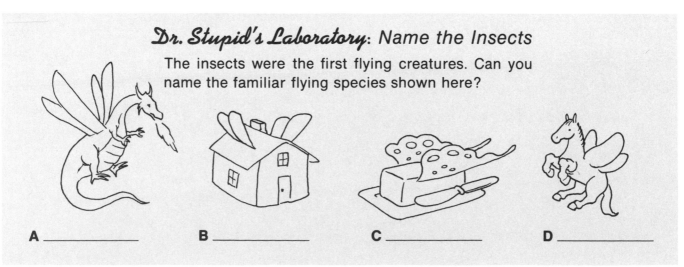

Dr. Stupid's Laboratory: Name the Insects

The insects were the first flying creatures. Can you name the familiar flying species shown here?

A _____ B _____ C _____ D _____

The Mammals

The first mammals were tiny shrewlike creatures. They seemed to be no match for the mighty dinosaurs. But though small, they were clever, and may have contributed to the downfall of the giant reptiles.

One of the mammals' evolutionary advantages was that they bore their young alive. As research has conclusively shown, animals that bore their young dead generally got nowhere.

The Age of Mammals

58

In winter, the mammals grew white coats with dark, numberlike markings.

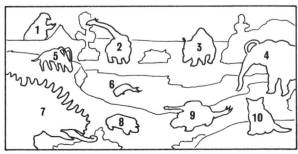

orthodont

The Rise of the Giant Mammals

After the Creosote extinctions, mammals were able to take advantage of the fact that they were **endothermic** (liked flowers), **placental** (had bad breath), and **quadrupedal** (didn't know any better) to spread and diversify.

In the Tutelary, mammals became the dominant class, and became quite large. The great Irish bunny, for instance, often had antlers eight feet across.

great Irish bunny

duck-billed mastodon

Megabrontotherium metamaximus Schultzi

The largest land animal of all time was *Megabrontotherium*. Standing 12,000 feet high at the withers, its shadow alone weighed 500 pounds.

Professor Schultz and workmen excavating toenail of *M. metamaximus*, at Devil's Grant Proposal National Wasteland, Wyoming, 1911.

Radiation of the Equids

The development of the horse is a good example of an evolutionary family tree. Starting with the tiny *Itsyhippus,* horses developed into a wide variety of larger species.

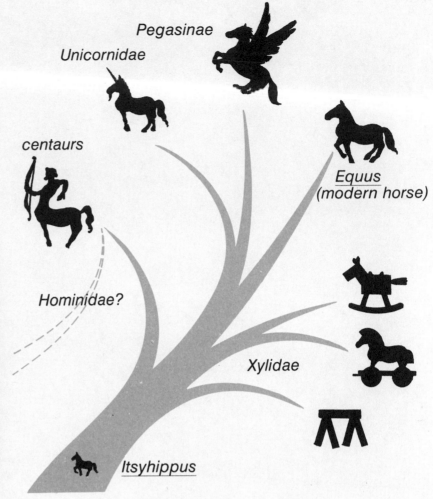

Pegasinae

Unicornidae

centaurs

Equus (modern horse)

Hominidae?

Xylidae

Itsyhippus

Seagoing Mammals

Like the reptiles, some mammals returned to the sea.

And some, after returning to the sea, even returned once more to the land!

sepentiforms

cetaceans

pinnipeds

land whales

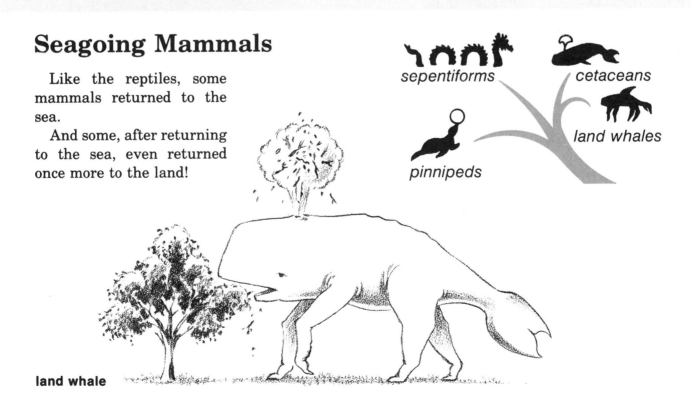

land whale

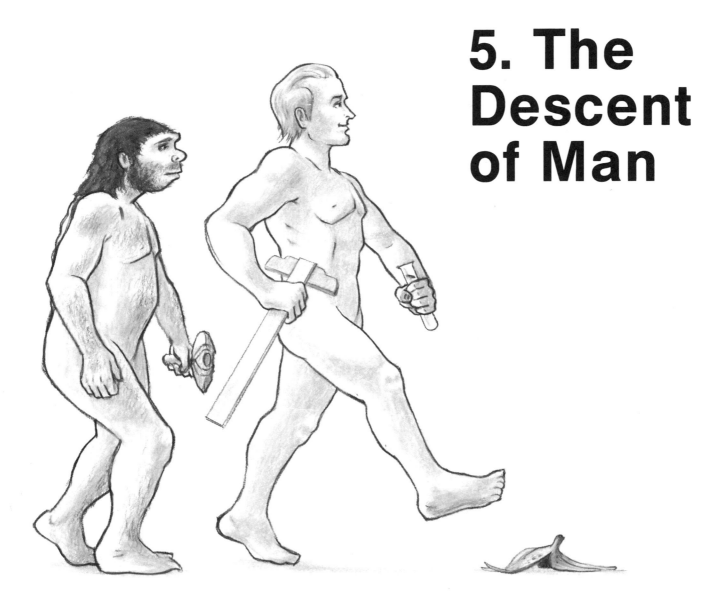

5. The Descent of Man

Lamarck

Darwin

Bonzo

Creationism vs. Evolutionism

There are still differences of opinion about the descent of man. In the past, there have been bitter disputes over what doctrines should be taught, especially in the public schools.

Today, however, we understand that all theories should be given equal weight and taught side by side. Accordingly, we will outline the two schools of thought and demonstrate the advantages that result from this evenhanded approach.

Moses

Savonarola

1-800-338-3030

Dr. Gene Scott

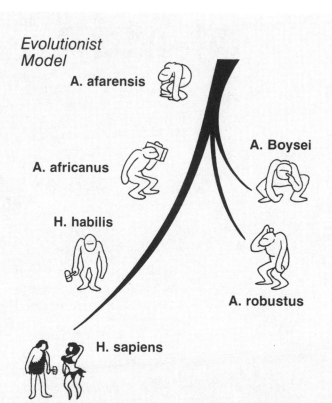

Evolutionist Model

A. afarensis

A. africanus

A. Boysei

H. habilis

A. robustus

H. sapiens

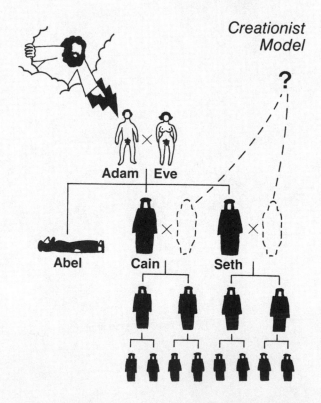

Creationist Model

?

Adam | Eve

Abel

Cain | Seth

This model demonstrates how the ancestral ape-men could have evolved an upright stance and a humanlike physiology. However, it does not explain the tremendous expansion of the brain—that most characteristic human feature.

This model explains the advent of human intelligence by ascribing it to divine fiat in the creation of the first humans, Adam and Eve. A major weakness is that it fails to account for the origin of Adam and Eve's daughters-in-law.

Evolutionist Method

Evolutionists hold that man arose by the same evolutionary process as other creatures, from early apelike ancestors.

This belief follows from the principle that the same laws of nature apply to man as to the rest of the physical world.

Creationist Method

Creationists believe that man was instantaneously created by God, based on an account in a book called "the Bible."

Several thousand years ago, a small tribe of ignorant near-savages wrote various collections of myths, wild tales, lies, and gibberish. Over the centuries, these stories were embroidered, garbled, mutilated, and torn into small pieces that were then repeatedly shuffled. Finally, this material was badly translated into several languages successively.

The resultant text, creationists feel, is the best guide to this complex and technical subject.

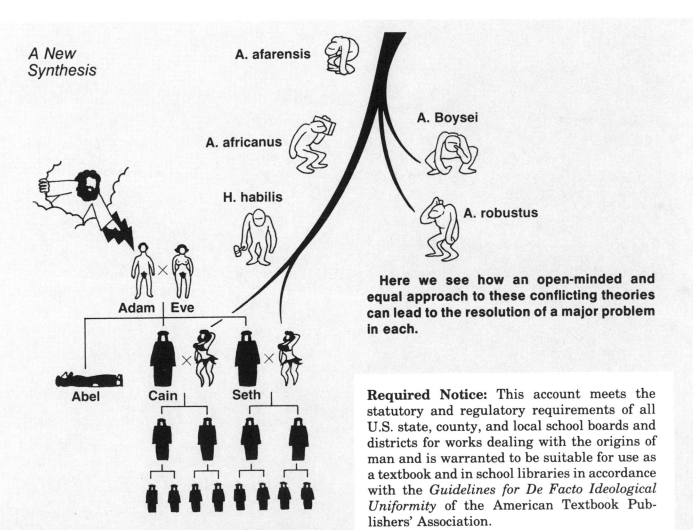

A New Synthesis

A. afarensis

A. africanus

A. Boysei

H. habilis

A. robustus

Adam × Eve

Abel   Cain   Seth

Here we see how an open-minded and equal approach to these conflicting theories can lead to the resolution of a major problem in each.

Required Notice: This account meets the statutory and regulatory requirements of all U.S. state, county, and local school boards and districts for works dealing with the origins of man and is warranted to be suitable for use as a textbook and in school libraries in accordance with the *Guidelines for De Facto Ideological Uniformity* of the American Textbook Publishers' Association.

Early Man

There were many "missing links" between the earliest ancestral apes and modern *Homo sapiens*. Scientists learn about these extinct species from fossil remains.

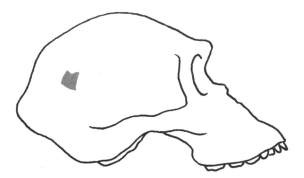

Reconstructed view of Desi skull; actual fossil remains are shown in color.

Here is an example of a fossil found near the famous "Lucy." It is the skull of an australopithecine male, called "Desi." Another couple named Fred and Ethel were found in a nearby cave, but Desi is the best-preserved specimen.

Scientists can learn much from a relatively small fragment of skeleton. From this fossil, it was deduced that Desi stood about four feet seven inches tall, walked with a slight limp, disliked zucchini, and was a registered Democrat.

Ask Dr. Stupid

Am I a Neanderthal?

Good question! As you know, Neanderthal man may have interbred with modern man. His descendants are with us even today, passing for full-blooded *Homo sapiens*. If you suspect a "touch of the old hand ax" in your ancestry, score yourself on this test:

1. Do your eyebrows meet in the middle? If so, give yourself five points.
2. Can you lock your knees in an upright position? If not, take five points.
3. Got a chin? If the answer is no, add three points.
4. How about a forehead? If not, add another three points.
5. Is it easy for you to balance a book on your head? Then give yourself five points.
6. Do you ever open Coke bottles with your teeth? If you do, add ten points.
7. Are you frequently more comfortable squatting on your heels than sitting in a chair? Take five points.
8. Is your head attached vertically to your neck? If not, add one point for every five degrees of slope.
9. Less than five feet tall? Add one point for every inch under.
10. If your lower arm is shorter than your upper arm, add one point for every inch of difference.
11. Ditto for your lower and upper legs.
12. Pigeon-toed? Five points.
13. Have you ever felt like bashing a postal clerk with a club? You're normal—no points.
14. Is the space between your big toe and your other toes big enough to hold an apple? Add five points.
15. Do you regularly eat apples in this way? Add fifteen points.
16. Do people think you're wearing your hair in a bun when you're not? Give yourself ten points.
17. Can you count your vertebrae while wearing two sweaters and an overcoat? Take five more points.
18. Is your nickname "Duke," "Butch," or "Animal"? Three points.

SCORING **0–20 points:** You are a virtually pure *Homo sapiens*. Feel free to build bridges, compose symphonies, and overrun the world. **20–40 points:** A slight Neanderthal strain means that you will occasionally have spells of primitive behavior, crawling around on all fours and whooping wildly. If you live in California, no one will notice. **40–60 points:** You can still function quite well in the modern world, but avoid eating in fancy restaurants lest your table manners give you away. **60–80 points:** Your Plasticine heritage is predominant. You should consider a career in pro football. **80–100 points:** Unfortunately, your genetic makeup is Grunt City; there is no place for you in human society. Try running for public office instead.

Java man

Peking man

Solo man

Piltdown man

Early Men

67

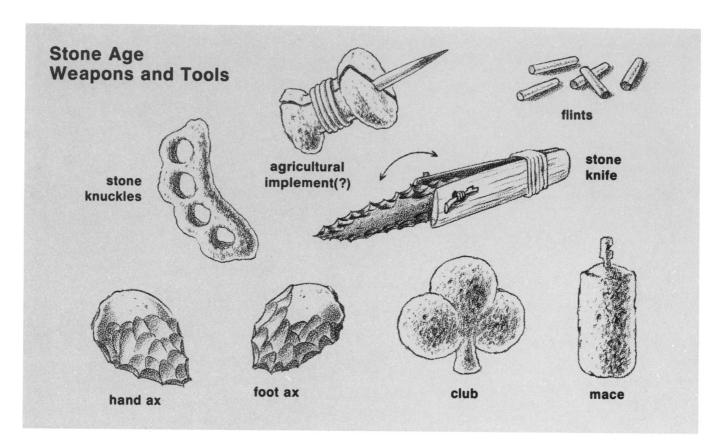

Stone Age Weapons and Tools

flints

stone knuckles

agricultural implement(?)

stone knife

hand ax

foot ax

club

mace

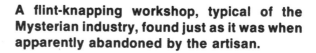

A flint-knapping workshop, typical of the Mysterian industry, found just as it was when apparently abandoned by the artisan.

Early *Homo sapiens* may have needed his weapons for defense against the savage Saber-toothed Man.

An exciting incident in the Upper·Paleolithic. ▶

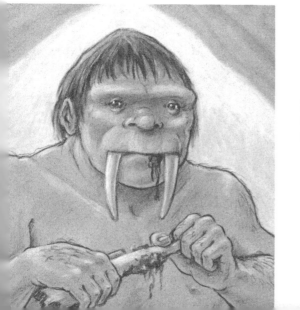

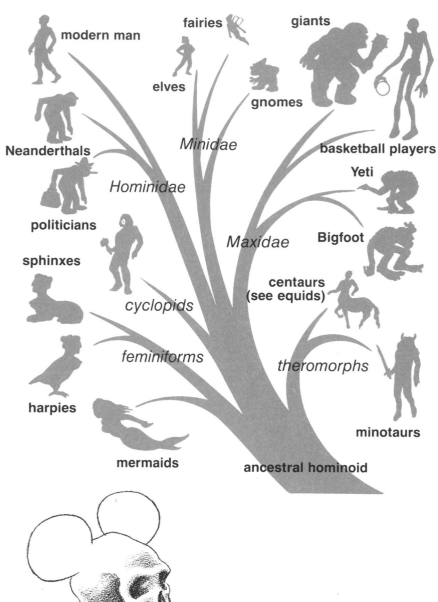

modern man

fairies

giants

elves

gnomes

Neanderthals

Minidae

Hominidae

basketball players

Yeti

politicians

Maxidae

Bigfoot

sphinxes

cyclopids

centaurs
(see equids)

feminiforms

theromorphs

harpies

minotaurs

mermaids

ancestral hominoid

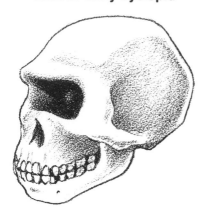

skull of early cyclopid

Nature's Misteaks

Men and the modern apes are not the only families that descended from the ancestral primates. Many early branches of the hominoid tree are now extinct, or survive only in isolated habitats.

Other fossil remains have yet to be reliably interpreted.

unknown hominid skull

Unusual skull and associated artifacts excavated at Devil's Running Gag State Useless Area, Wyoming.

Unsolved Mysteries

This reconstructed specimen has defied classification, even as to order.

Paleolithic cave art, like this example from Oeufs en Cocotte, France, may have been used in magical rituals. Note how the sophisticated execution of the figures transcends the crude composition.

A magician as reconstructed from representations in cave art. In primitive society, the shaman combined the roles today divided between the stage magician, the artist, and the technician: making valuable objects disappear, usually into his own pocket.

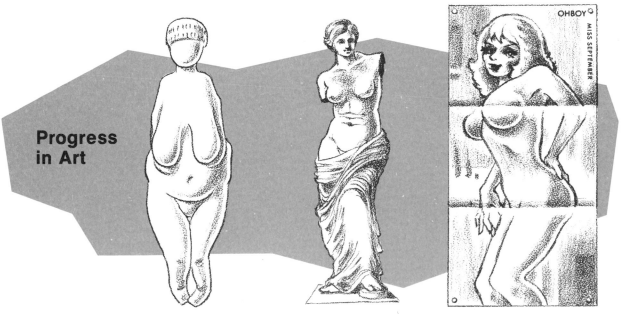

Progress in Art

30,000–10,000 B.C.   SECOND CENTURY B.C.   SEPTEMBER 1984

The Advance of Civilization

THE ZIGGURATS The Great Ziggurat of Ur is one of the masterworks of early civilization. The ancient people who built these structures have long since vanished. This suggests that ziggurats may be dangerous to your health.

DESERT LINES In the Peruvian desert, the ancient inhabitants created huge patterns of lines, visible only from the air. The purpose of these great works remains a mystery. If they were flying-saucer landing strips, as has been suggested, why are there no nearby remains of parking lots or Hiltons?

THE PYRAMIDS The pyramids at Giza were one of the wonders of the ancient world. Here they are shown with the original façades restored. We do not know the significance of the black markings, referred to in hieroglyphs as "the Eyes of the Snake."

STONEHENGE Computer analysis of this structure has shown that the weight of its stones, in ounces, is precisely equal to the number of stars in the universe! It is shown here as it may have looked in use. Similar studies are under way at other sites, such as Brickhenge, Stuccohenge, and Masonitehenge.

The Noble Savage vs. Civilized Man

Primitive man lived an idyllic existence, in harmony with nature and his fellows. The advance of civilization exacted a price: as the old ways were replaced by the new, tribal man forgot his ancient, natural wisdom.

Among the tribal traditions often displaced by the encroachment of modern society were:

slavery
extreme subjugation of women
fishing by poisoning rivers
human sacrifice
continuous intertribal warfare
hunting by driving herds of animals off cliffs
ritual mutilation
extreme xenophobia
abandonment of the old and dying
cannibalism

Despite these losses, civilization brought many benefits. Among them were:

slavery
extreme subjugation of women
air, water, and soil pollution
organized crime
continuous international warfare
organized religion
fast food
traffic
street mimes
blow-in cards

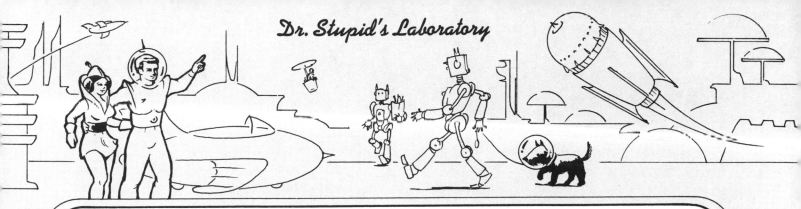

Wonderful Future Invention Checklist

Science is sure to bring us even greater technical marvels in the years to come. Save this page as your own personal record of scientific progress. When you get your first household robot or take that trip to Mars, write the date in the appropriate blank. (At some point, of course, you may want to transfer your checklist to a molecular hologram in your skull-implanted computer.)

Invention	Date	Invention	Date
HOUSEHOLD ROBOT	_____	FIRST WOMAN PRESIDENT	_____
PERSONAL AIRCAR	_____	FIRST BLACK PRESIDENT	_____
PERSONAL SUBMARINE	_____	FIRST _____ PRESIDENT	_____
SPACE STATION	_____	FIRST _____ PRESIDENT	_____
SPACE COLONY	_____	ENGLISH CHANNEL TUNNEL	_____
PERSONAL ROCKET	_____	TRANSATLANTIC TUNNEL	_____
ATOMIC ROCKET	_____	SPACE WAR	_____
FOOD IN PILL FORM	_____	ONE WORLD STATE	_____
MAGNETIC TRAIN	_____	FLYING SAUCER LANDS	_____
ATOMIC DIRIGIBLE	_____	Name of alien(s) _____	
FLAT-SCREEN TV	_____	INVASION BY SPACE ALIENS	_____
FLAT-SCREEN 3-D TV	_____	Name of aliens _____	
THEATRICAL HOLOGRAPHS	_____	CURE FOR CANCER	_____
HOME HOLOGRAPHS	_____	CURE FOR COMMON COLD	_____
FEELIES	_____	CURE FOR _____	_____
TWO-WAY WRIST RADIO	_____	CURE FOR _____	_____
TWO-WAY WRIST TV	_____	X-RAY SPECS	_____
RAY GUN	_____	FLOATING CITIES	_____
INTELLIGENT COMPUTER		UNDERGROUND CITIES	_____
(passes Turing test)	_____	ANTI-GRAVITY	_____
ANDROID	_____	FASTER-THAN-LIGHT DRIVE	_____
MY TRIP TO MOON	_____	MATTER TRANSMITTER	_____
MY TRIP TO INNER PLANET		INVISIBILITY	_____
Mercury	_____	UNIVERSAL LANGUAGE	_____
Venus	_____	Name of language _____	
Mars	_____	WORLD WAR III	_____
MY TRIP TO OUTER PLANET		WORLD WAR IV	_____
Jupiter	_____	WORLD WAR V	_____
Saturn	_____	WORLD WAR VI	_____
Uranus	_____	ACCESS TO OTHER	
Neptune	_____	DIMENSIONS	_____
Pluto	_____	TIME MACHINE	_____
Planet X	_____	TRACTOR BEAM	_____
MY TRIP TO OTHER SYSTEM		FORCE SHIELD	_____
Name of star _____	_____	IMMORTALITY	_____
MY TRIP TO OTHER GALAXY		SPELLING REFORM	_____
Name of galaxy _____	_____	CALENDAR REFORM	_____
INSTANT ACCESS TO ALL		DYSON SPHERE CONSTRUCTED	_____
HUMAN KNOWLEDGE	_____	PHYSICAL INSTRUMENTALITY	
HUMAN CLONES	_____	ABANDONED	_____
WEATHER CONTROL	_____	ENTROPY REVERSED	_____
MILE-HIGH SKYSCRAPER	_____	NEW JOKE INVENTED	_____

Appendix

The appendix is a wormlike organ connected to the large intestine. It has no known function and is considered the vestigial survival of a former digestive process.

In man, the appendix is found at the bottom of the caecum, a pouchlike swelling of the large intestine where the small intestine empties into it. It is around one-half inch thick, and varies from one-half to eight inches in length. The inner lining, or mucosa, is continuous with the intestinal lining. The mucosa is covered by the epithelium, the muscle coat (which gives the organ its capacity for peristalsis), a layer of connective tissue, and finally the visceral peritoneum.

Digestive matter flows into the appendix from the intestine and is forced back by peristaltic contractions. Appendicitis is the result of a blockage that prevents this evacuation, the trapped matter inside the organ then producing infection.

The appendix occurs in man, a few mammals such as rabbits and Old World porcupines, and books.

Glossary

atomic pile   a painful condition in atoms

Avogadro   a vegetable used in guacamole

Brownian motion   the movement of microscopic particles caused by Brownies

chromatic aberration   wearing brown shoes with a blue suit

circular reasoning   *see* reasoning, circular

epoch   the sound made by a hen

half-life   Saturday night in Fresno

hyperbola   an ellipse as described by Howard Cosell

Loschmidt's number   (415) 767-1678

mantissa   a female mantis

midden   a kind of fingerless glove; often, **kitchen midden**   a glove worn for protection from hot utensils

Milky Way   a commercial confection

milliHelen   the amount of beauty required to launch one ship; 1/1000th of a Helen

ohm   where the art is

programmer   a person with a natural sense of algorithm

quark   the sound made by a durk

radiocarbon dating   a courtship ritual among archeologists

reasoning, circular   *see* circular reasoning

Roche's limit   three beers

semiconductor   a part-time employee on a streetcar

three-body problem   the problem faced by a triple murderer in hiding the evidence

unit of power   watt   **I said, unit of power**   watt   **I SAID . . .**

Suggestions for Further Reading

General

The One-Minute Scientist   Franklin Pierce Dong
Zen, Cocaine, and Science: An Incoherent Metaphysical Babble   Wolf T. Swedenborg
Thinking on the Wrong Side of the Brain   Tuesday Kurosawa

The Universe

Let the Stars Guide Your Divorce   Sheherazade O'Feeny
Build Your Own Comet Shelter   Gepetto F. X. Esterhazy
Weight Loss Through Space Travel   Rolf Birdseye, D.D.S.

Matter and Energy

Special Relativity for Special Children   Zenobia Mintz Bender
General Relativity for Generals   Bomilcar Toth
Sight Without Glasses Through Magnetism   Wolfram Tungsten
"Nuclear Power Killed My Poodle," *NoEvolution Quarterly* No. 37, Treemonisha Pancake

The Earth

Geology—Fact or Fancy?   Tor Rotweiler
Our Friends the Rocks   Emma Firebaugh Treehouse
Make Your Own Back-yard Volcano   Rex Y. Teabucket
Rocks from Outer Space   Zbigniew Farquhar
Continental Drifter   Faron "Poker Slim" Kallikak

Evolution

Finding Fossils in Your Attic   Epaminondas Millefiore
Dinosaurs from Outer Space   G. Kingsley Firpo
My First Book of Endothermic Therapsids   Maude Dingle Winterhalter
Evolution, A Communist Lie   Col. Tubalcain Billy Snowbird, U.S.A.F. (ret.)
Endangered Animals with Big Brown Eyes   Erasmus M. N. Braithewaite

The Descent of Man

They Walked Sort of Like Men   Rae Dawn Schicklegruber
A Field Guide to Western Girls   Nils Van Der Whoop
Man the Toolbreaker   Constance d'Annunzio Blight
The Picture Book of Racial Degenerates   Norman and George Lincoln Rockwell

METRIC UNITS OF MEASUREMENT

Prefixes		Name	Description
10^{12}	helluva-	arg	unit of work performed incorrectly
10^{9}	heckuva-	galumph	unit of waste motion
10^{6}	lotsa-	lumpen	unit of resistance to getting out of bed in the morning: = gravity × inertia × apathy
10^{3}	buncha-		
10^{2}	bozo-	fignewton	= 100 calories
10	decca-	jowl	unit of excess weight: = lumpens × fignewtons
10^{-1}	desi-	melvin	unit of temperature, as measured from absolutely perfect to absolutely awful
10^{-2}	sexi-		
10^{-3}	silli-	yok	unit of humor
10^{-6}	pismo-	vampire	unit of repulsive force of garlic
10^{-9}	banana-	candelabra	unit of tasteless interior decoration
10^{-12}	doodoo-		
10^{-15}	nono-		
10^{-18}	nada-		

SYMBOLS USED IN MATHEMATICS

⋛ greater than, less than, or perhaps equal to
∿ has some kind of relation to
≢ is very reminiscent of
⍨ probably has nothing to do with
⫝̸ is too expensive
⩭ must be equivalent to something
α⌇ x varies as y, or maybe z
⩲ plus or minus an unknown sum
⩵ I'll let you know when I look it up
∪ I left the figures in my coat pocket
Ʒ some
⊛ pie
⟁ what's the difference?

CONVERSION TABLE FOR WEIGHTS AND MEASURES

Length

325 cubebs = 1 furbish
6 furbishes = 1 nautical smile
20 nautical smiles = 1 minor league
3 minor leagues = 1 major league

Liquid Measure

24 pips = 1 damn
6 damns = 1 merkin
$9\frac{1}{2}$ merkins = 1 galleon
1.2 galleons = 1 empirical galleon

Dry Measure

6 grits = 1 scrimmage
$4\frac{1}{2}$ scrimmages = 1 hogsnout
3 hogsnouts = 1 ratsass
12 ratsasses = 1 passel

Weight

24 carrots = 1 pickleweight
30 pickleweights = 1 tuna
1000 tunas = 1 short ton
1.37 short tons = 1 tall ton

POWERS OF TEN

10^{18}	1 heavy year, in meters
	1 light year, in meters
10^{16}	
10^{14}	
	Distance from Fresno to the Sun, in meters
10^{12}	Distance from Fresno to anywhere, in meters
10^{10}	Number of Big Macs served to date
10^{8}	Baseball player's salary, in dollars
	Best-selling author's royalty, in dollars
10^{6}	
10^{4}	
10^{2}	
	Average author's royalty, in dollars
10	
	Thickness of slice of veal scaloppini, in meters
10^{-2}	Thickness of slice of prosciutto, in meters
10^{-4}	
10^{-6}	Probable value of rare stamps found in attic, in cents
10^{-8}	
	Probable value of unsolicited advice, in cents
10^{-10}	
10^{-12}	
10^{-14}	
	Diameter of banker's heart, in meters
10^{-16}	Diameter of graphic designer's brain, in meters
10^{-18}	Diameter of politician's integrity, in meters

PRONUNCIATION SYMBOLS USED IN THIS BOOK

ḃ	*as in*	bdellium	h́	" "	humble	p̃	" "	comptroller
b̅	" "	dumb	h̊	" "	ghost	r̈	" "	February
c̃	" "	cnemis	k̂	" "	know	ŝ	" "	island
d̦	" "	Dneiper	Ī	" "	half	ś	" "	Illinois
d̦	" "	djinn	m̈	" "	mnemonic	t̆	" "	rustle
e̯	" "	home	n̂	" "	damn	t̂	" "	boatswain
g̈	" "	gnu	o̦	" "	serious	w̃	" "	boatswain
g̅	" "	align	p̦	" "	pneumonia	x̊	" "	Sioux

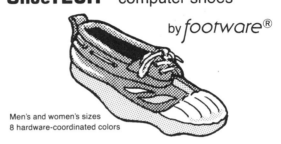